blud

blud

Rachel McKibbens

COPPER CANYON PRESS

PORT TOWNSEND, WASHINGTON

Cover art: August Natterer (1868–1933), *Meine Augen zur Zeit der Erscheinungen* (*My Eyes in the Time of Apparition*), undated, Inv. No. 166, ©University Hospital Heidelberg, Prinzhorn Collection

Copper Canyon Press is in residence at Fort Worden State Park in Port Townsend, Washington, under the auspices of Centrum. Centrum is a gathering place for artists and creative thinkers from around the world, students of all ages and backgrounds, and audiences seeking extraordinary cultural enrichment.

LIBRARY OF CONGRESS CATALOGING-IN-PUBLICATION DATA

Names: McKibbens, Rachel, author.
Title: blud / Rachel McKibbens.
Description: Port Townsend, Washington : Copper Canyon Press, [2017]
Identifiers: LCCN 2017022743 | ISBN 9781556595240 (paperback)
Subjects: | BISAC: POETRY / American / Hispanic American.
Classification: LCC PS3613.C559 A6 2017 | DDC 811/.6—dc23
LC record available at https://lccn.loc.gov/2017022743

COPPER CANYON PRESS
Post Office Box 271
Port Townsend, Washington 98368
www.coppercanyonpress.org

How many people will be sleeping in the old houses
the night when my hair lets out tongues of its fire
and burns everything to the ground?

—Diane Wakoski

Contents

I

II

III

IV

blud

I

the first time

I came back to life
was in 1980.
I awakened

head a blue
labyrinth
trapped in sound—

a grotesque clutter:

the meep-meep of a
cartoon bird

sticky flock
of children
screeching
in the courtyard.

Then a voice
(voices?)
I did not
recognize:

the ruined gasp
emerging from
within
my cutoff throat.

I unwrapped
the telephone cord—
how long had I been

down?—skull
fever-pounding
from the blackout,
body feathered in sweat.

I listened
to the room,
felt the rush
& shuffle
of my heart—
a felled finch.

Lavender shock
of resurrection.

Lucky my dad
was not awake
to find me there—

his radiant little
death inventor
with X'd-out eyes,
a halo of birds
circling my dome.

Lucky to have
outlived this
unripened error.

Can you imagine it?
A child standing
at the mouth
of the underworld

pleading
for a time-out,
trying to reason
with whatever's
in charge:

No, no! I never
meant to stay dead.
I simply wanted
a sweeter life.

a brief biography of the poet's mother

There was
a child
hemorrhaging
light,
the blue song
of her brain,
an early maggot
writhing.

Her mother,
a jealous
newlywed,
with looking-glass
hands & a tub
full of bleach

thieved & thieved
until the child
became
a quiet room

a silence born
of interrogated
flesh.

Girl is the worst season.
Mother no guarantee.

No clothes or meat,
no heavy tit wrecked
with milk.

So the blue song
became a dirge,
then the dirge
became a girl.

maybe this will explain my taste in men

When Dad busted my face open
I got to stay home from
school, watched cartoons
all day like a goddamn king.

Dad called in sick,
icing his damaged fist
with frozen peas & meat.
Overheard him on
the phone with his boss:

Broke my hand yesterday
playing ball with the kids.
Can you believe it?
I caught a fastball, no glove.
My own damn fault.
I'll get those blueprints
to you tomorrow morning,
first thing.

Poor Dad. When he hung up
he squeezed my shoulder
& winked. Just after lunch,
there was a knock on the door.

I peeped through the blinds
with my one good eye, saw
a blonde in a nurse's uniform.

Dad opened the door & howled
as she sang him a high-pitched
song, bending at the waist
to show off her tits.

At the end of it, she handed him
a catcher's mitt with a
get-well card.

The boys at the office
sure look after me!
he roared, shaking his
head in disbelief
then handed me
the remote so I,
too, could
know love.

poem written with a sawed-off typewriter

Some of us vanish
out of habit, guided
by some blood-orchestral pulse—
the delirium chorus
of a rowing mind.

She was always going.

I haven't seen her
in two decades
& I have felt
every year.

What's the word
for a shadow's
shadow? Apparition,

dark twin, heartless
daughter?

Sometimes she calls
on your birthday,
my father says.

Confused.
Her mouth full of radio wire.

God is a signal, the devil a song.

*

Hey Ma, how many voices
does it take for a schizophrenic
to change a lightbulb?

Wait. I'm sorry.

Let me ask
an easier question:
When you left,
did you leave
your children
half-full
or half-empty?

three strikes

After Uncle Phil got
eight years
for coke possession
I inherited his bedroom,
a modest kingdom
magnificent in its starkness:

ball chain hanging
from exposed lightbulb,
narrow mattress
& weight-lifting bench,
its iron rings laced in dust.

Nights my struck face
throbbed, when
my body swelled blue
from every pore,
I'd lie in bed
& pray to vanish

closed my eyes
so tight I saw stars.
I wanted to become
the reversal of light,
to exist
only within the
hard-clenched black—

kindergarten pariah
with a sweet tooth for death.

There, at the end
of a smoke-stained

hallway, I discovered
the women,
bodies shelved
above the unworn
coats & flannel
button-ups.

Kitty. Crystal.
Heather. Ashley.
Vicky. Candy. Kim.

Feathered hair
& lip gloss,
pussies held open
by French manicures

they instructed me on
the body's forbidden dialect,
the gospel of ecstasy,
how heat can ravage
from the inside out.

I'd practice in the closet.
Masturbated in the bathroom stall
at recess. Deep
in my sleeping bag
during slumber parties.
The Sunday school
cloakroom. Dentist's
office. The backseat.
My middle finger,
a shriveled magician.

How else could I survive
the endless winter

of my childhood?
Hell-spangled girl
spitting teeth into the sink,
I'd trace the broken
landscape of my body
& find God
within myself.

the sandbox

for Lisa or Laurie

We held each other / in silence / mouth against mouth / blood & thunder
scorching the grass / Behind the shed / I played the husband / brutish
breadwinner / choking her flesh / in my troubled hands / pulling her head
back / to lick / from neck to ear / in frenzied thrill / The kind of love / I
learned from movies / & what light swamped the air / as I shoved my bald
pelvis into hers / blood ripening into wolf brine / burning a girl-shaped
hole in the clover? / Every afternoon I became a god reinventing sky /
expert forger of the dry hump / I asked *Who's your daddy?* before that was
even a thing / Once the recess bell rang / I released her back / into the
quiet unwild / to no-longer-mine / to fat white tubs of minty paste / &
songs about Jesus / From across the room / I watched my bride / make
eyes / with the real boys / & knew I could kill for her / drill a body down
into the earth / boy in the Polaroid / a grisly figurine / The white horse of
masculinity bucking wild on the inside / I bit my lip & did as I was told /
After school / I wanted / to hold her hand / she always wanted a divorce /
When the big kids followed me home / calling me / *lesbo / homo / wetback /
faggot* / I held my chin out & challenged to fight them all / every time /
& why not? / Might as well / we all knew / I would never / win / anything.

leverage

Before the burglar
raped my grandmother

he pushed her down
a flight of stairs.

Ankle turned, hip unhitched.
There was no getting up, no

hope for flight. She told me that while he
was on top of her, she stared up

at the clock from the kitchen floor.
Watched each minute crawl by

like a half-smashed bug,
imagining the school bus

emptying her sons into the yard.
Thought of the sandwiches

she had no time to make.
As the man pulled his pants up,

she noticed the tattoo on his
forearm. MOTHER framed

by a heart. *My sons will be home
soon*, she explained.

How many?
Five.

What she told me next
I could never understand,

not until I'd lived long enough
in this temporary body,

not until I had five children
of my own, how, when the man

held out his hand, she took it.
Neither of them speaking as she

leaned all her weight onto her one
good foot, the two of them standing

in the kitchen, spreading butter
onto bread.

letter from my heart to my brain

It's okay to hang upside down
like a bat, to swim
into the deep end of silence,
to swallow every key
so you can't get out.

It's okay to hear the ocean
calling your fevered name,
to say your sorrow is an opera
of snakes, to flirt with sharp
& heartless things.

It's okay to write,
I deserve everything!
To bow down
to this rotten thing
that understands you,
to adore the red
& ugly queen of it, admire
her calm & steady rowing.

It's okay to lock yourself
in the medicine cabinet,
to drink all the wine,
to do what it takes
to stay without staying.

It's okay to hate
God today, to change
his name to yours,
to want to ruin all
that ruined you.

It's okay to feel
like only a photograph
of yourself, to need
a stranger to pull
your hair & pin you down,

it's okay to want
your mother
as you lie alone
in bed.

It's okay to brick
to fuck to flame
to church to crush
to knife to rock
& rock & rock
& rock
& rock & rock
& rock.

It's okay to wave
goodbye to yourself
in the mirror.

To write, *I don't want anything.*
It's okay to despise
what you have inherited,
to feel dead
in a city of pulses.

It's okay to be the whale
that never comes up
for air, to love best
the taste of your
own blood.

letter from my brain to my heart

This house is dirty
but comfortable.
Behind each crooked door
waits the angry weather
of a forgiveless child.

I cannot help but admire
this horrible power
of mine, how each small thing
can become a death:

the lost house key,
a spoiled egg, a howling dog.

There is no prayer
or pill for this.
It is a ruthless botany.
I might as well
be buried in the yard.

I have no one to blame.
Not the mother
who sang to an
empty cradle.

Not the Dogs of Spite
who bit my hand,
just this long-legged sorrow
who trails
my every joy
like a dark perfume.

You have my permission
not to love me. I am
a cathedral of dead bolts
& I'd rather
burn myself down
than change the locks.

ghost town

A cold witness, she sits.
   My unbeloved mother—

trapped daughter
   of my bright asylum.

I am never alone, peer
   into the left eye of me

& you will find her squatting
   face knifed & dim

hair scribbled over
   that big yellow grin.

The mirrors, deviled in shit,
   grind her face into

the meat of me. Pale, pale, I eat
   abandoned houses

to keep her fed,
   give her spoiled milk

until her teeth go dead.
   She tumors me a song.

It would take a gun to birth her.
   O bullet, O midwife!

Draw the lunatic out,
   throw that voice

slanted with madness into
      the cemetery air.

Give me a field of rotting crows
      & I will bury her there.

II

drought (California)

Once they've rid their bodies

    of an impossible country,

        become flatbed livestock

in migration,

    you coin them not of this earth.

Beings of neither flesh

        nor light

    *

        When I was small

    I saw men & women—brown terrestrial bodies—

bent in the field

      a mile

from the strawberry stand

    in ninety-five-degree heat

one hundred

      one hundred & three.

I'd ask my father

    to stop the car

to gobble each sunlit jewel,

adorn my mouth

      in bleeding seeds

NO

   he'd answer   sharply

as if their sweat

      contagious

      *

When the woman at the taqueria

     attempted

to speak to me (in audible hieroglyphics)

   I knew it was

   something mine   but not mine.

     No habla español   my father said

my closed mouth

    a thorn

      shoved hard into her lip

    *

When my great-great-grandparents

     arrived from Guanajuato,

they wore no disguises—Mercedes

    vibrant

in a handmade dress,

Pedro (my father's namesake)

in a silent

gentleman's hat.

Did they, too, imagine

becoming ghosts

like I have,

like I do?

Boneless satellites in lace

swaying above

their children's heads?

If no child of mine

becomes a poet

will the absence of my tongue   shimmer

like betrayal

in their mouths?

heretic

If, by lineage,
our children are
doomed to orbit
this spoiled delirium

to flag the creeping world
where I was born
& have been killed
so many times

if the man in white
is right, if the weight
of this melancholy
makes a black hole
of me

& the faces I once carried
become planets
I can no longer name

tie my hair
to the bedposts, love,
tuck their baby teeth
beneath my tongue,
then cut, cut, cut

until my blood
becomes a door.

Dawson, NM. 1905

Night awakens,
or someone's mouth
& out steps
blood & marrow
in a dress. A long
wool thing. Dead brass
watch on a flat-boned wrist.

With a hiss of braids
coiled atop her head,
an infant girl strapped
to her chest, she arrives.
As whole as a woman can be.

Here she is permitted
the soft pleasures
of the ordinary:

pale grit of masa
spread quickly
into husks,
the calloused edge
of her husband's hand.

Settling into this
foreign kingdom
there is no need
to daydream,
no chore
interrupted.

Praise the tender
asylum of repetition:
dishes cleaned,
then stacked.
Skirts hemmed,
floors swept

the New Mexican
soil still intact,
unmined,
still something
like a gift.

Her healthy daughter
dreaming in milk,
gentle husband
not yet charred

why, then, would she
notice the crows
gathering like germs
on her porch,
their dark throats
chilling the air
with a cold
death noise?

outhouse

for Jacob

What does the god of your childhood look like?
      A soft apparition pigeoned in the attic,

a wound eating you one year at a time? If you could
      destroy the story before it started, would you—

go back—before the unnameable thing?
      If you could return to your father at the foot

of the bed, would you swallow your sisters whole to save them?
      Obedience in the wrong house is a kind of plague,

survivor's guilt a sleight of hand. No outrunning
      your blood's calamity, so you gather your teeth

& dig your trenches, tell your stories but never come clean.
      No news from the mother yet. Just your gutted sisters

embalmed in the outhouse. Your ageless smile going bad
      in a frame.

the second time

was in my classmate's
mouth. Lying on

the floor of her baby blue
bedroom she asked,

*Do you think
you're a boy or a girl?*

& everything inside
me came bruising

to the surface.
Neither, I said

& it was understood.
In that charged silence,

she rolled over, draped
her wronged body

over mine, as if to anchor
the damaged bastard

with no desire to stay.
She listened to the awakened

heat of me, its bright
song infecting my blood.

Our feral bodies, driven
by unmothered chaos

returned each other to
the living. All hail

the power of a proper
finger fuck & the wet

demolition of shame.
What I had once

mistaken for death
was, instead, a door.

the ghost's daughter speaks: white elephant

she won't be attending my party　　　she's an astronaut　　　always in
orbit　　she can't come to the phone　　　　she's making dinner　in the
shower　　　　at a very important meeting　　She's asleep &
we were warned　　　not to wake her　　　　She can't come to　　my recitals
since the explosion　　　that was her　　on television　in the big　　white
　　　　smoke　　　my mother's name is　　　　　　my mother's name
　　　was　　　Judith Resnik　yes, the astronaut　　　　　not the teacher
one　　　　　　　the pretty one
We　　aren't allowed　　to answer the phone　　　　can't write our name on
the mailbox　　　　　　　We aren't supposed to　　　answer the door
when　　Dad's　at work　can't open　　　the windows　　the curtains
　　　　　　our mouths　If she finds us　　she might　　　　she will
　　　One day she's　　going　　　　to
We have a code: ring once　then　　hang up　call　back　　let it ring two
times　hang up call back　　then maybe we'll　　answer　　We aren't
　　　　　allowed to　　　　　　play outside anymore
　　　　　Grandma accidentally said　*A n a h e i m*　so she's here　　now
　　somewhere　　searching for our　　mailbox　　　we can feel it
　　　　we can smell　　　her hair　She is going　　　to find us
again　　Peter,　if you sneak outside　　you have to　　knock
　　to be let back in　　knock three　　times　　if you're alone
four　with a　space between the　third　& fourth　knocks　　if she's
standing behind you　　　The judge says　she's allowed　visitation again
　　　　she's better now　　　believes in　God　says
I'm going　　　　　　　　to　hell　　because I touch my
　　privates　　says she knows　I speak
to the devil　knows　he gives me orders　through my headphones
She made me stand　naked　&　spread　　used the handle　of her
　　　　toothbrush　to look inside　for roaches　　she says
　　because　　I'm Mexican　　　　　I'll have　a lot of
　　roaches　　　She took me　to see　Billy Graham

at   Angel Stadium   to get born again   she needed to start

     over   because her   stepdad   touched inside her   She keeps

lots of   dead   cats in her freezer   says if I'm good   &

    pray   they will come back to   life & be my pets

      I named   all six of them first   so Peter   can't

say any are his   Our mother   never sleeps   we've been warned

      not to wake her

    but if she never   sleeps how can we   not wake her?   She says she

was   mad   when   I was born   she wanted only boys   she

      named the   little boy inside   her but then   she buried

               him

She told   the lawyer   she can feel where the Germans stuck needles

    in her stomach

      Please delete   my maiden name

please don't   post it on the internet   my mother   is so many people

      & all of them will find me

    my mother is   not well   there's   something   wrong

with   She hasn't been okay since   She's never

They say she can't   They say   batshit   psycho

        cuckoo for Cocoa Puffs

        She says I'm going to pay for

what I've written   I'm going to pay for this poem

        She has a way

of making things

      happen

  Please   quit saying   *but she's your mother*

    I've never

     We've never

         had

    You don't know

what it's   like
I   don't think   you're

   listening

You   don't

                              understand

                                        that bitch is
                                        Kray.*

---

* Twin brothers Ronald "Ronnie" Kray and Reginald "Reggie" Kray were notorious gangsters in London's East End during the 1950s and '60s. Ronnie was rumored to have suffered from paranoid schizophrenia and was later judged to be criminally insane and spent thirty years in a secured mental hospital.

weight

He interrupted winter with his own.
Over chocolate cake & Jimmy Stewart
I got the news. Couldn't stay

on the phone long, no room
left in me for the shaming
language: *Stupid. Selfish. Waste.*

Over time it became *the accident*,
too drunk to count all the pills
he'd taken. No need to unbury
the tragedies of lineage.

What was in the blood stayed.

Mudstruck veins, shot liver
& all that dark honey
chalked up to shit arithmetic.

Gilbert, sweetest uncle,
saddest *vato* on the block,
moved back in with his parents
the only summer he wasn't locked up.
His PO warned it was the worst
place to stay clean.

Loaded on whiskey & H,
he played guitar one night
while his mama
scorched the air in protest

howling in the wake of her son's
audible grief, the inconvenient
drawl of requiem.

Each song pulled from him
like something stolen,
Gilbert sang until the starless night
caved in on itself, each note
a wounded calf limping
across the floorboards.

Mama! Mama! You never loved us,
did you? Mama, why didn't you try?
he sang, in the greenest
voice ever invented.

I watched as she stood there
silent in the doorway,
Gilbert reaching for her
like a child beckoned
by a cursed spindle.

Without offering the grace
of a single word
she turned her back to him,
strolled into the kitchen
& turned the radio on.

word problem

Pictured is The Mother you have neither seen nor spoken to in twenty-three years. The total of this absence amounts to 8,400 days of CrushingLoss®.

If the memory develops three holes for each day of CrushingLoss, what is the total number of holes The Mother's memory has accrued if each hole splits in two every seven years?

Show your work.

kin

In January
when nothing could thaw

my son confessed
he wished me dead.

Then, piled in the center
of the attic floor,

a most cruel jackpot:
every gift I'd ever given him,

a diary of fang & venom.
The trees, crippled by ice,

stood watch as my son
moved slowly down

the street like a hearse.
Then, gone.

All winter, I wanted to
write a poem that did not

involve the word *ruin*.
My body. This house.

The child who refused
to take hold. Such desperate,

complicated thefts.
Pry my mouth open

find the stench
of a final prayer:

Dear Gods of Flesh
& Instinct,

Forgive my boy's inherited crimes—
the voices that spin

his brain into a wooden
horse. Grant him

a warm home, far away
from this body.

My blood has never been
& will never be
                    kind.

oath (blud litany)

If your ma's got an alias for each voice & all six have hungered for you
        so long you had to change your own name
                if your son awakened last winter a dark carpenter
                        unhammering the knots from his veins

if your parents dug a four-foot hole in the yard to spill a boy into
        if you yearn to uncover the glory of your sickness
                to polish every inch of it, spit-shine & marvel
                        if you've named your head *a glistening chaos*

instead of *drowning in bad animal light*, if your bl__d gives your children
        & your children's children a gift that seems to take & take & take
                & take & take & take & if your flesh can't resist
                        the unshut maw of an awful god

if you know by heart the pros & cons of slashing your throat
        versus slashing your thighs, if you fear your hands
                will become your body's assassin, if all your meds
                        put together amount to a carry-on,

if you're always willing to risk more than what you've been given,
        if you wake up feeling empty & struggle to allow this emptiness
                to be a comfort as you lie still within the soft forgotten witch
                of your body

if this makes you scream out *holy shit what if maybe today I am fine*
        if you've ever searched for mercy in the sharpened hands
                of an I-told-you-so, if your name is the song
                    of a dark water muse calling you down

into its muddy tapestry, we are kin / *familia* / familia(r) / B-L-U-D
blud fanged & one-voweled, the thick & heavy. simple.
from out the mud we siren eternal
blud royals of lost skin & shadow

I unbl__d you to blud you. blud the terror echoes of heredity.
blud each bruised memory into weightlessness. blud beloved.
blud hum / blud the ready ghosts of shame
blud possess your body back to holy

blud thrive / blud rush / blud bone menagerie / blud wild / woke
horse / fang / laced / covet / slick / gut / wing / lit
blud full moon hustle & oath.

*   *   *

To my daughters I need to say:

Go with the one who loves you biblically.
The one whose love lifts its head to you

despite its broken neck. Whose body
bursts sixteen arms electric

to carry you, gentle
the way old grief is gentle.

Love the love that is messy
in all its too much. The body

that rides best your body, whose mouth
saddles the naked salt of your far-gone hips,

whose tongue translates the rock language
of all your elegant scars.

Go with the one who cries out for her
tragic sisters as she chops the winter's wood,

the one whose skin triggers your heart
into a heaven of blood waltzes.

Go with the one who resembles most your father.
Not the father you can point out on a map,

but the father who is here, is home,
the key to your front door.

Know that your first love will only be the first,
& the second & third & even fourth

will unprepare you for the most important:
The Blessed. The Beast. The Last Love

which is of course the most terrifying kind.
Because which of us wants to go with what

can murder us? Can reveal to us our true heart's
end & its thirty years spent in poverty?
Can mimic the sound of our bird-throated
mothers, replicate the warmth of our brothers'

tempers, can pull us out of ourselves until we are
no longer sisters or daughters or sword swallowers

but instead women who give & lead & take & want
& want
& want
& want

because there is no shame in wanting. & you will
hear yourself say: Last Love, I wish to die

so I may come back to you new & never tasted
by any other mouth but yours & I want to be the hands

that pull your children out of you & tuck them
deep inside myself until they are ready to be

the children of such a royal & staggering love.
Or you will say: Last Love, I am old & I have

spent myself on the courageless, have wasted
too many clocks on the less-deserving, so I hurl

myself at the throne of you & lie humbly
at your feet. Last Love, let me never

roll out of this heavy dream of you, let the day
I was born mean my life will end where you end

let the man behind the church do what he did
if it brings me to you. Let the girls in the

locker room corner me again if it brings me
to you. Let this wild depression throw me beneath

its hooves if it brings me to you. Let me pronounce
my hoarded joy if it brings me to you.

Let my father break me again & again if it
brings me to you.

Last Love, I have let other men borrow your children.
Forgive me.

Last Love, I once vowed my heart to another.
Forgive me.

Last Love, I have let my blind & anxious hands
wander into a room & come out empty.

Forgive me. Last Love, I have cursed the women
you loved before me. Forgive me.

Last Love, I envy your mother's body
where you resided first. Forgive me.

Last Love, I am all that is left. Forgive me.
I did not see you coming. Forgive me.

Last Love, every day without you was a life
I crawled out of. Amen.

Last Love, you are my Last Love. Amen.
Last Love, I am all that is left. Amen.

I am all that is left.
Amen.

III

one more time, with feeling

When I was nineteen
I stole a gun. The drug dealer
next door, blitzed out
of her skull, didn't
see me
pull it from her
kitchen cupboard.

As the California sun
sank below the
foothills, I haunted
the neighborhood,
screaming your
doomed name.
I was ready.
A death-wish Romeo
beneath your bedroom
window. Split once
a neighbor threatened
to call the cops.

I never told you this story.

Not because I regret
what I did, was prepared
to do—those forty-five
minutes of havoc, hunting
down your head.

Back then, I wasn't shit.
Just electrified violence.
All fists, piss & safety pins,

an unwed teenage mother
with no address.

You had parents. Freckles.
A three-story house. I'd listen
to you spit your angsty
fiction while I slept in parks
& ate from garbage cans.

When I learned you were
coveting the man I loved,
I felt my insides darken,
cursed your well-fed
royalty disguised as grit.

Got tired of the forgery,
wanted all the black-eyed
wealth to myself:
BANG, you're dead.

Wish I could say I've put
those days behind me,
that I never fall into
the steel-weight daydream
of a gun's hard lesson.

1995—half my life ago—still,
every time you call
to bitch about your latest
ex-soulmate or DUI,
one more kid taken
from you by the state

I want to tell you
about the only night

you survived.
When something
said *fall asleep*
& you did.

Crashed hard
with a starving bitch
& pistol at the ready,
birds still singing
in the half daylight.

I'll say it here, right now,
one more time, with feeling:
it was the only moment
in this wretched life
a god was on my side.

deeper than dirt

after the poet asked how I would bury my brother

Beyond the carrots
& blind white worms,
beyond the yellowed bone
orchards & corkscrew roots,
beyond the center of this
churchless earth

beloved Peter, my little sorcerer,
brought up dirty & wrong,
you deserve more
than to be smothered in mud.

For all the gravel you were fed,
for every bruise & knot
that named you
I must plant you in a quiet bed
of blood-hot muscle

deliver you into me,
so I may carry you as
the only mother
we have ever known.

singe

My trust
is always
measured
by what
you've lost—

how many
dresses
have you
put into
the ground?

How many
fresh-bought
suits?

What needed
killing
for you to
become?

Loss is never
just loss.

I want
your blood
to have
sharpened
from it

need to know
you responded
animal

hurled your
demented
body
into
the river
spitting out
the ghosts
of their
dead names.

sermon

Each time I see a woman
walking in a grocery store

or sitting on a bench
in a park or a funeral parlor,

I want very much
to taste the woman,

lick every blessed
inch of her from the

bottom of her calloused
heel to the top

of her glorious head.
If she is wearing an eye patch,

I want to lift its smooth
& sleeping lid,

whisper something sweet
beneath it, push my tongue

around its spoonlike edge.
If the woman is older,

I want to taste the history
carved into her flesh,

learn each translucent hair
of every fragile limb.

If she is missing a breast,
I want to taste the bright

& rugged scar of it,
press its ghost-soft nipple

against the bridge of my
mouth. If she is a mother,

I want to soothe her many hands,
trace each silver bolt of

childbirth etched along
her torso, taste the salted

hole of her, this sacred,
this blood-hot church.

una oración (bruja's soliloquy)

I arrived one body-part at a time.
First, the scalloped middle,

blue-roped torso. Eyes, nose & ears,
blood-licked. Then the blur of this electric mouth,

the wet unfolding of my arms, legs & fists.
The last, of course—this cauldron of a cunt.

The nurses delivered me to my parents
on a dinner plate. Father howled.

Mother thinned down to a milkless shadow.
I have always been a god-hammered girl.

Dirty as a turnip, I crawled into
the blind center of the earth

a worm built to outlast the swallow.
When I was young, I kissed the girls too hard,

riddled my tongue with a father's profanity—
I thought this was how to become a boy.

Bent daughter of a six-fisted man,
I wanted the safety of a cock. Permission

to roar. Dumb as the moon, I knew
nothing of this body

other than the violence it ignited,
how my bones reeked of motor oil—

my every opening a socket to blacken
each thieving finger.

Who would ever choose to be
the damaged house?

Better to be the demolition gender.
Cinder block & dog-rotted

I strutted the world. Turned the mirrors
& swore off every version of myself.

It wasn't until the third
time my body was taken

from me I learned how to love it.
Now I walk the streets

forcing men into uncomfortable eye
contact: You wanna fuck with me?

I wanna fuck with you.
What greater burden, what more

unconquerable revolt is there than that
of a resurrected woman?

Ripe with vengeance, I termite.
Tomorrow I'll button my blouse

with a dozen kitchen knives &
cast your dreamless skulls

into the cemetery soil
& that's just breakfast.

I own my blud. What you borrowed
I will come back for.

Scratch your name into a coffin nail,
bind it in hair & wax

an ungentle ceremony
for your ungentle hands.

O captive, my captive!
I have coined your suffering song,

have driven you back into your
hellish light.

Let the drilling of the worms
be your only sermon,

the wasting of your flesh
a salvaged psalm.

Listen: anything holy
is not reversible.

There isn't a man alive
who could undo me.

swell

I have never had a mother, or, no longer have

      or, once did, briefly, for a day or two.

         Perhaps she was only mine

during the wet crown of hours I spun my skull

      through her ripe & widening cunt,

         then fastened to her nipple—

a botched daughter ugly with hunger.

      Or maybe it was long before the orphaning,

         before the womb fell quiet & her brain

went sour—gentle reader, won't you permit me

      this sweetness?—the morning she straddled

         my father, a black flood of hair,

throat opened to God, the red muscle of her quickening

      like the pulse of a dazzled child. Yes,

         let it be there, in that heat-ravaged

moment as she caught the pale bloom of herself

      in the mirror & looking

         back over her shoulder,

fell in love with the animal engine of her body,

not for the daughter it could nurture,

but for the girl it would kill.

fairy-tale pantoum for my seven-year-old self

after Wallace Berman

The queen is dead. The queen is dead. The queen is dead.
The queen is dead. The queen is dead. The queen is dead.
The queen is dead. The queen is dead. The queen is dead.
The queen is dead. The queen is dead. The queen is dead.

The queen is dead. The queen is dead. The queen is dead.
The queen is dead. The queen is dead. The queen is dead.
The queen is dead. The queen is dead. The queen is dead.
The queen is dead. The queen is dead. The queen is dead.

The queen is dead. The queen is dead. The queen is dead.
The queen is dead. The queen is dead. The queen is dead.
The queen is dead. The queen is dead. The queen is dead.
The queen is dead. The queen is dead. The queen is dead.

The queen is dead. The queen is dead. The queen is dead.
The queen is dead. The queen is dead. The queen is dead.
The queen is dead. The queen is dead. The queen is dead.
The queen is dead. The queen is dead. The queen is dead.

The queen is dead. The queen is dead. The queen is dead.
The queen is dead. The queen is dead. The queen is dead.
The queen is dead. The queen is dead. The queen is dead.
The queen is dead. The queen is dead. The queen is dead.

The queen is dead. The queen is dead. The queen is dead.
The queen is dead. The queen is dead. The queen is dead.
The queen is dead. The queen is dead. The queen is dead.
The queen is dead. The queen is dead. The queen is dead.

The queen is dead. The queen is dead. The queen is dead.
The queen is dead. The queen is dead. The queen is dead.
The queen is dead. The queen is dead. The queen is dead.
The queen is dead. The queen is dead. The queen is dead.

salvage

I have learned to need the body
I spent years trying to rid the world of

have learned to cherish its pale rebel hymn
warped by ghost heat, carried, carried

by all my loyal dead. I have learned
to crawl backward into the wilderness

to ask, to eat, to steep in your gentleness.
Let this be where I permit forgiveness

to know your name, to leave our cruelest years
where & how we need them most—

behind & unlit.

for Carol, who is no one

Mother, you lousy walk-on.
      You muddy old bitch.

I've become your good daughter,
      I have written you a part

big as the Mississippi, I have authored
      you a new womb filled

like a gas chamber. Here is your
      fat mouth brimming with

pills. This is no poisoned apple
      movie-star spell, Mother.

You still are what you are: a plotting
      mirror-bitten hag

who hobbles the halls like a jilted
      landlady, babbling on & on

about your ghost-skinned girl.
      Your angry daughter.

Your bad invention. Where did you
      go for so long?

Why did you leave us alone with
      the woodsman?

Do you know I have five dizzy
      dwarfs of my own?

They have heard all the stories.
      They know your real

name: *Carol! Carol!* We sing
      knots into your hair

& piss on your soap. We've built
      you a castle covered in

witches & if you should come,
      dear Mother, to visit us

we will serenade your face with
      a choir of hammers.

Feed you to the river in a dress
      made of stones.

glutton

you write poems to understand what you cannot understand. finally name the snapping beast you've tried to outrun your entire life. stop avoiding. stop the scorched fog of language that redirects the eye. say what you mean. quit saying *better* when you mean *eviscerated*. lunacy is in your blood. it's a fact. so you do your best to live alongside its snarl. push & push until you find room in that frantic brain to plant some kind of hope: your daughter upstairs, practicing the clarinet. this morning's toast, its butter spread all the way to the edge. small mercies to help empty the beast. so why is it, every time you write about your son, the boy who hears voices & voices & voices, he responds, sends a message out of the blue? it makes you worry maybe you're on the same frequency. worry tomorrow you'll wake up like him. like the woman who birthed you: tiny ghost pulled from a bigger ghost. you know better. language is a conjuring, lineage the cruelest coven. your boy feels you writing him from three thousand miles away. perhaps he lives in your head the way your mother lives in your head. even now, after all these years, you say her name aloud & her hair grows another three inches. it's a fact. your boy starts each message off okay. *hi mom, I love & miss you so much!* the relief (he's alive! coherent!) will last a few seconds, a minute tops, before he starts spilling out a jarring sequence of words that demand you go a little more crazy to understand them. but you refuse. you want to stay here, don't want to be what he inherited from you & isn't that the worst thing you have ever written? boy of your flesh & mottled blood. threatened you & his siblings. promised to kill you & wrote exactly how. & these were bottomless, devastating moments, yes, but nothing in the world readies you for today's gutting. when you ask if he's okay, is he warm, does he have anyone to talk to. when you make yourself ask him, do you have any friends? all the swirl & dodge collapses & he says, simply, *no. I don't have any friends.* & you want to jump off the bridge upon learning this. you want to chop off your hands. he is small again, first grade, waiting in the office with his head down. the principal is telling you a kid from class was picking on him. she doesn't have to tell you who it was. you know the one.

Brad. the big, husky prick who regularly punches your boy in the back of the head & calls him *faggot*. Oh, if only madness walked home down Newport Avenue like Brad did that day. if only you could grab madness by the face & hold it against a chain-link fence, a few yards from where a group of teenagers are playing kickball. if only you could look it in the eye & hiss *you touch my kid again, I will stomp your fucking life out.*

IV

my eyes in the time of apparition

Curse the steady mice who feast upon
        my son's gray matter—

            those soft purveyors of wickedness,
       mutilators of my womb,
    mutilators of an empty chapel.

Praise the sirens of widening synapses,
     who beckoned my boy to fall,
        then drift, upstream

           to sleep without song & awaken
               savant: a piano angel hypnotist,
         miracle hands
       fraught with confessions,
    their ivory lament.

Blessings to this illness that sutures mother
       to daughter to son & back.
          Bless sorrow's commitment
              to reincarnate—an infant's
         familiar arrival—a cold boy
      sprung from the witch's head.

Curse America & its willful gatherers
       of foul seed & excess, castrators
          of dreams, vengeful shepherds
              of paranoia. Curse you curators
        of shame,
      of ridicule, of my eager impermanence.

Praise the mayhem of my prefrontal cortex—
            psycho bitch brain fluke,
                        most divine imaginer!
                                    Praise my eyes in the time
            of apparition, each heretic winter,

        as my teeth spark, igniting
the darkening litany of genetics
            & growl: *Let me be what I am.*

dead radio apostle

Heels in stirrups,
knees pitched
above my hips,
I am blinded
by every
measured breath
required before each push—

a cold, unnatural
discipline.

I was taught
to focus
on something
in the room,
to distract from
the hell-rigged pain
knifing me
from the inside.

I study the 9
on the clock,
its spine curved inward,
quiet as a stillborn,
as the doctor waits
at the mouth of me.

Womb knuckled
by spark & spasm,
I hold the nurses' faces,
a gallery of stunned
amazement—their wet eyes

& ruptured mouths,
then push.

A red howl tongues
the air. The doctor grips
a handful of black hair.
An inch. An inch.
An inch. Three feet.

The nurses tilt their bodies
in unison, a chorus
of gathered weight.
Wrenched fists
yanking loose
the skull that splits me.

I have ridden the Lord
into salvation,
my mother shrieks,
shouldering
through my pelvis.

Deliver me, O Lord,
from the blood
of the lamb!
she sings
as her bad brain
enters the room.

The nurses lock hands
around her waist
& pull. A blackbird
on the window's ledge
pecks the flesh
of a rotted peach.

Lord, I have siphoned
the devil from
my children's mouths,
I have throned their unholy
bodies in shit!

I push again, beyond
the thickening fog of voices,
delivering my mother
into an unrelenting light.

The nurses drag her
to the cleaning station.
Her voice pools
at their feet,
wavering in lost pitch.

They wipe down
her shrinking body,
suction pearls of mucus
from her nose & throat.

She writhes on the table,
cold & unnamed.
Then lessens.
Smaller & smaller still,
until her body
is swaddled
in a washcloth
& placed in my hands.

She blinks me
into focus & the room

is bewitched,
a museum of blood
& silence.

I rock her in my palm—
the last blue pill
in the bottle—then
shove her into
the nest
of my missing tooth.

I sing a song to the
emptied room.
I rise three feet
above my bed.

the last time

I did it alone.
Not in bed
where I'd willed
myself dead
so many years
I became
apparition

not in the bathroom
where I fed my body
to a hungry blade &
cut down my hair
with a match.

It was not in the arms
of the man I tried
over & over to amputate

or in the songs of my
kind & clever children.

No.

The last time
I came back to life
was in the middle
of an ordinary day,
while at the grocery store,
when I caught
my reflection
in the butcher's glass
& did not
flinch.

the other children have agreed to forfeit their inheritance

When it comes,
we do our best
to declare
NO VACANCY

ignore its rotted
knock when, say,
my tomato sauce
spills upon
the tablecloth

& my brain
responds the only
way it is wired
to respond—

the dizzy spiral of
a hypnotist's wheel,
hair lifting wicked
from my scalp.

Quickly, my girls
wet the cloth
with salt. Quickly,
my boy spoons
out another dish.

Let us pretend,
for a moment,
this won't ever end:
the relentless
machine of us.

Let us defy
the laws
of science
& inevitability,
say

we will go on
even as all
the poisons
of the house
reside in me,

when madness
knows no other
name but mine,

we will go on.

Acknowledgments

Heartfelt gratitude to the editors of the journals that first published poems from this book, some in slightly varied forms:

Academy of American Poets Poem-a-Day, *Affilia: Journal of Women and Social Work, Apogee, The Bakery, Best American Poetry* blog, *Boaat, Imaniman: Poets Writing in the Anzaldúan Borderlands, The Literary Review, Muzzle Magazine, Scoundrel Time, Stone Canoe, Tandem: Volume 1, VIDA: Her Kind, Vinyl Poetry, Winter Tangerine.*

Deepest love and appreciation to all who helped drag this book out of me: Jacob Rakovan, Piper Jane Austin, Christina Perez, April Jones, Airea D. Matthews, Ada Limón, Rachel Wiley, Amy and Matt Law, Patricia Smith, Jan Beatty, Richard Blanco, Amber Tamblyn, Brenda Shaughnessy, Dominique Christina, Casey Rocheteau, Marta, David, Frenchie, Alan, Ricardo, and Stephen.

My sight has been sharpened by the work, love, and community dedication of Britteney Black Rose Kapri, Sonya Renee Taylor, Nicole Homer, Terisa Siagatonu, Mahogany L. Browne, Porsha O., Charlotte Abotsi, Justice Gaines, Chrysanthemum Tran, Venus Selenite, Porsha Rashidaat J. Olayiwola, Giselle Robinson, Miriam Harris, The Dark Noise Collective, and the Pink Door coven.

I raise a fist in solidarity with all who live with mental illness and all who have voiced demands to be seen and understood and loved and honored. We, the most feral singers, we who open our throats to swallow the sky's shimmering and perfect darkness, we are so goddamn holy.

Notes

"the sandbox" is for all fellow humans who have managed to unhitch themselves from the gallows of toxic masculinity.

"leverage" is dedicated to my late grandmother Priscilla Cordova Camacho and to the quiet women/femmes. *La casa no descansa en la tierra sino en la mujer.*

Both "letter from my heart to my brain" and "letter from my brain to my heart" are dedicated to the students of PS 811 M.

"ghost town" was influenced by an old Mexican proverb, "Breed crows and they will take your eyes out."

"drought (California)" is dedicated to the memory of my ancestors, Mercedes and Pedro Rodriguez Sr., who emigrated from Guanajuato, Mexico in 1905 with the hope of finding a better life. In October 1913, Pedro, along with more than two hundred fifty immigrant miners, perished during an explosion in the Dawson, New Mexico, Stag Cañon Mine No. 2.

"heretic" is based on the medical research that suggests bipolar disorder is a cause of dementia.

"the second time" is dedicated to Kim G., whom I treated poorly due to my own self-loathing and internalized homophobia. Wherever you are, I hope you are surrounded by gentleness.

"weight" is in loving memory of my uncle, Gilbert Luis Camacho.

"word problem" owes a great debt to the following mathletes who figured out the answer: Kyle Macey, Jesse Parent, Spencer David Retelle, Rik Andes, Ronnie K. Stephens, Jenise Michele Frangella.

"oath (blud litany)" is for all my blud kin. May we live and live and live and live.

"deeper than dirt" owes its life to poet/activist Denise Jolly.

"glutton" is for Anthone, my one. I will curse the lineage and burn down the worlds of all who seek to harm you.

"my eyes in the time of apparition" borrows its title from the painting by German artist August Natterer.

About the Author

Rachel McKibbens is a two-time New York Foundation for the Arts poetry fellow and the author of *Into the Dark & Emptying Field, Pink Elephant,* and the chapbook *Mammoth.* In 2012, she founded the annual Pink Door Writing Retreat, open exclusively to women/femme/trans/nonbinary writers of color. She lives in upstate New York.

Poetry is vital to language and living. Since 1972, Copper Canyon Press has published extraordinary poetry from around the world to engage the imaginations and intellects of readers, writers, booksellers, librarians, teachers, students, and donors.

WE ARE GRATEFUL FOR THE MAJOR SUPPORT PROVIDED BY:

THE PAUL G. ALLEN
FAMILY FOUNDATION

CULTURE

Lannan

OFFICE OF ARTS & CULTURE
SEATTLE

  SEATTLE FOUNDATION

TO LEARN MORE ABOUT UNDERWRITING
COPPER CANYON PRESS TITLES,
PLEASE CALL 360-385-4925 EXT. 103

WE ARE GRATEFUL FOR THE MAJOR SUPPORT PROVIDED BY:

Anonymous

Jill Baker and Jeffrey Bishop

Donna and Matt Bellew

John Branch

Diana Broze

Sarah and Tim Cavanaugh

Janet and Les Cox

Mimi Gardner Gates

Linda Gerrard and Walter Parsons

Gull Industries, Inc. on behalf of
Ruth and William True

The Trust of Warren A. Gummow

Steven Myron Holl

Phil Kovacevich and Eric Wechsler

Lakeside Industries, Inc.
on behalf of Jeanne Marie Lee

Maureen Lee and Mark Busto

Rhoady Lee and Alan Gartenhaus

Ellie Mathews and Carl Youngmann
as The North Press

Anne O'Donnell and John Phillips

Petunia Charitable Fund and
advisor Elizabeth Hebert

Suzie Rapp and Mark Hamilton

Joseph C. Roberts

Jill and Bill Ruckelshaus

Cynthia Lovelace Sears and
Frank Buxton

Kim and Jeff Seely

Catherine Eaton Skinner and
David Skinner

Dan Waggoner

Austin Walters

Barbara and Charles Wright

The dedicated interns and
faithful volunteers of
Copper Canyon Press

Lannan Literary Selections

For two decades Lannan Foundation has supported the publication and distribution of exceptional literary works. Copper Canyon Press gratefully acknowledges their support.

The Chinese character for poetry is made up of two parts:
"word" and "temple." It also serves as pressmark for
Copper Canyon Press.

The poems are set in Adobe Caslon Pro. Headings are set in Quarto.
Printed on archival-quality paper.
Book design and composition by Phil Kovacevich.

Printed in the USA
CPSIA information can be obtained
at www.ICGtesting.com
JSHW080717050924
69294JS00002B/5

9 781556 595240